LEVEL
3

Water

Melissa Stewart

NATIONAL
GEOGRAPHIC

Washington, D.C.

For our watery world,
thanks for making life possible —M. S.

The publisher and author gratefully acknowledge the expert review of this book by Willem H. Brakel, Ph.D., Department of Environmental Science, American University.

Paperback ISBN: 978-1-4263-1474-2
Reinforced library edition ISBN: 978-1-4263-1475-9

Book design by YAY! Design

Photo credits
AY: Alamy; GI: Getty Images; NGC: National Geographic Creative; SS: Shutterstock
Cover, VladisChern/SS; 1, Corbis/SuperStock; 2, David Deas/DK Stock/GI; 4-5, WorldSat International Inc./Science Source; 6, Dennis Kunkel Microscopy, Inc./Visuals Unlimited/Corbis; 7, Phil Degginger/Carnegie Museum/Science Source; 9, Martin Barraud/Stone Sub/GI; 10, Elenamiv/SS; 11 (UPLE), Greg Amptman/SS; 11 (UPRT), FLPA/AY; 11 (CTR), Brian J. Skerry/NGC; 11 (LOLE), Dante Fenolio/Photo Researchers RM/GI; 11 (LORT), Emory Kristof/NGC; 12, David R. Frazier Photolibrary, Inc./AY; 13, Renato Granieri/AY; 14 (UPLE), Brian Lasenby/SS; 14 (UPRT), trainman32/SS; 14 (LO), Solvin Zankl/naturepl.com; 15, Gail Shotlander/Flickr RF/GI; 16-17, Ulrich Doering/AY; 18, Kennan Ward/Corbis; 19, NASA/Science Photo Library; 20 (LE), microcosmos/SS; 20 (RT), Dmitry Naumov/SS; 21 (UP), Leigh Prather/Dreamstime.com; 21 (LO), Stocksearch/AY; 22-23, pmenge/Flickr Open/GI; 24-25, Markus Gann/SS; 24 (UPLE), Shan Shui/Photographer's Choice RF/GI; 24 (UPRT), Sydneymills/SS; 24 (LOLE), Jamie Grill/Brand X/GI; 24 (LORT), Sinibomb Images/AY; 25 (UPLE), Pakhnyushcha/SS; 25 (UPRT), Peter Orr Photography/Flickr RF/GI; 25 (CTR LE), Kichigin/SS; 25 (CTR RT), Ladislav Pavliha/E+/GI; 25 (LO), Dennis Hallinan/Hulton Archive Creative/GI; 27 (UP), Mimadeo/AY; 27 (LO), Matt McClain/The Washington Post via GI; 28 (UP), swish photography/Flickr Open/GI; 28 (LO), Hellen Grig/SS; 29, JLImages/AY; 31 (UP), C_Eng-Wong Photography/SS; 31 (CTR), Holmes Garden Photos/AY; 31 (LO), Christophe Testi/SS; 32, AfriPics.com/AY; 34 (LE), Kenneth Libbrecht/Visuals Unlimited/GI; 34 (RT), Kenneth Libbrecht/Visuals Unlimited/GI; 35 (UPLE), Kenneth Libbrecht/Visuals Unlimited/GI; 35 (UPRT), Kenneth Libbrecht/Visuals Unlimited/GI; 35 (LO), Jim Reed/Science Source; 36, SuperStock; 38, Dennis Welsh/Uppercut/GI; 39, Images Bazaar/GI; 40-41, Bill Hogan/Chicago Tribune/MCT via GI; 42-43, Tim Pannell/Corbis; 44 (CTR), Elena Elisseeva/SS; 44 (LO), Igorsky/SS; 44 (UP), WorldSat International Inc./Science Source; 45 (UP), Can Balcioglu/SS; 45 (CTR LE), Monkey Business Images/SS; 45 (CTR RT), Andrey Armyagov/SS; 45 (LO), design36/SS; 46 (UPRT), ArtTDi/SS; 46 (CTR LE), Kennan Ward/Corbis; 46 (CTR RT), Stocksearch/AY; 46 (LORT), design36/SS; 46 (LOLE), holbox/SS; 47 (UPRT), gst/SS; 47 (CTR LE), microcosmos/SS; 47 (CTR RT), Renato Granieri/AY; 47 (LOLE), NASA/Science Photo Library; 47 (LORT), Can Balcioglu/SS; vocabulary boxes, kobi nevo/SS; top border, Maria Ferencova/SS

Printed in the United States of America
14/WOR/1

Table of Contents

A Watery World

Take a look at Earth from space. Why does our planet look so blue? It's blue because water covers almost three-quarters of Earth's surface.

Half of the world's plants and animals live in water. The other half depend on water to live and grow. Life as we know it couldn't exist without water.

About 326,000,000,000,000,000,000 (326 quintillion) gallons of water fill Earth's oceans, lakes, ponds, rivers, and streams.

The first life on Earth was tiny one–celled creatures that appeared in the ocean about 3.5 billion years ago. As time passed, these simple creatures changed and developed. They became larger, more complex creatures.

Scientists believe that the first life on Earth was tiny, one-celled creatures called archaea (AR-kee-uh). This photo, which was taken through a microscope, shows a kind of archaea that lives on Earth today.

This illustration shows just a few of the animals that lived in Earth's ancient oceans 600 million years ago.

The earliest animals probably lived about 600 million years ago. Eventually some animals left the water and moved onto land. But many animals and other creatures continue to live in Earth's oceans.

All About Oceans

Almost all of Earth's water is in its four huge oceans—the Atlantic, Pacific, Indian, and Arctic. All of the oceans are connected, and salty seawater is always on the move.

Earth's Ocean Currents

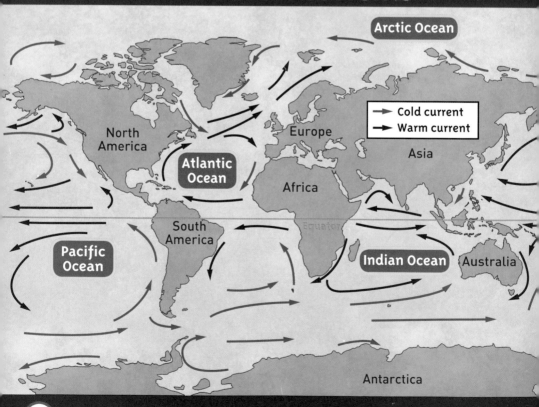

Arctic Ocean

North America

Europe

→ Cold current
→ Warm current

Asia

Atlantic Ocean

Africa

Equator

South America

Indian Ocean

Australia

Pacific Ocean

Antarctica

Deep cold-water currents flow across the ocean floor toward the Equator. Warmer water near the surface moves toward the North and South Poles.

Water Words

CURRENT: A flowing stream of water within a larger body of water

EQUATOR: An imaginary line around Earth halfway between the North and South Poles

Wavy Water

As the wind blows, waves form in the open ocean. When a wave gets close to shore, its bottom hits the shallow seafloor and slows down. But the top keeps going. This causes the top to fall over and crash onto land.

The top of this wave is falling over.

Scientists have explored less than one-tenth of the ocean's total area.

Look out across the ocean, and you see nothing but water and waves. But just below the surface, the ocean is teeming with life.

Deeper down, the water is pitch-black and freezing cold. But many creatures are able to live in these conditions.

bluestripe snappers

plankton

a manatee mother and calf

deep-sea cockatoo squid

deep-sea crabs
and tube worms

Quiet Waters

Unlike the salty ocean, lakes and ponds are filled with fresh water. These normally quiet bodies of water are fed by rivers, streams, or underground springs. They form in low areas of land.

Lake Superior is the largest lake in North America. It contains one-tenth of the fresh water on Earth's surface.

a glacier that still exists in Patagonia, Argentina

Many of the world's ponds and lakes formed in a surprising way. Thousands of years ago, Earth was very cold. Thick glaciers (GLAY-shurs) covered large areas of Europe and North America. As these ice sheets moved south, they scraped giant holes in the land.

Then about 11,500 years ago, Earth warmed up. Many glaciers melted, and their water drained into the holes to form lakes and ponds.

Water Word

GLACIER: A giant ice sheet that slowly moves out in all directions

Fish and frogs. Snails and turtles.
Ducks and dragonflies. These are just
a few of the animals that live in, on,
and around lakes and ponds.

A great egret catches its dinner.

As water plants soak up sunlight, they get energy to make food. Then they become dinner for insects, fish, snails, and ducks. And those animals are eaten by frogs, birds, and other predators. Quiet waters are the perfect home for all these creatures.

Go With the Flow

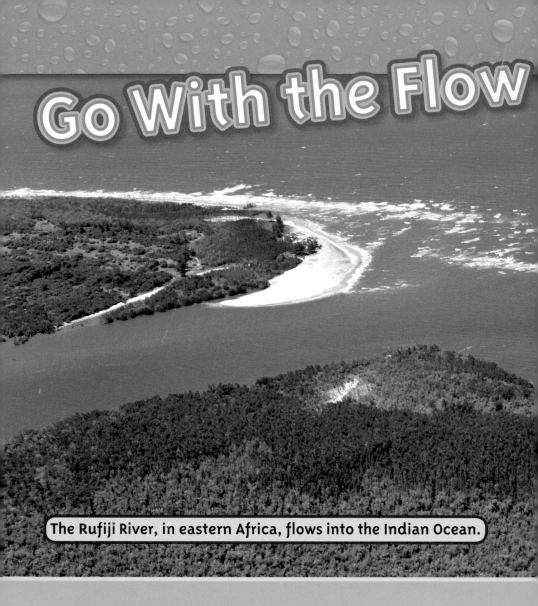

The Rufiji River, in eastern Africa, flows into the Indian Ocean.

As rain falls and snow melts, water flows downhill. It forms fast-moving streams that join together, becoming rivers. The water keeps on going until it reaches the ocean.

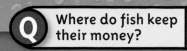

The kind of life in a river depends on how quickly its water flows. Plants can't grow in fast-moving water, but they have no trouble surviving in slower water. ... live in the areas of a river where ... find food.

As a river races across the land, it knocks loose bits of soil, sand, and rock. The fast-flowing water carries those bits with it. The water erodes riverbanks. It digs out river bottoms. Over time, the rushing water changes the shape of the land.

Over millions of years, the Colorado River has slowly eroded the rock around it. This is the most important force behind the formation of the Grand Canyon, U.S.A.

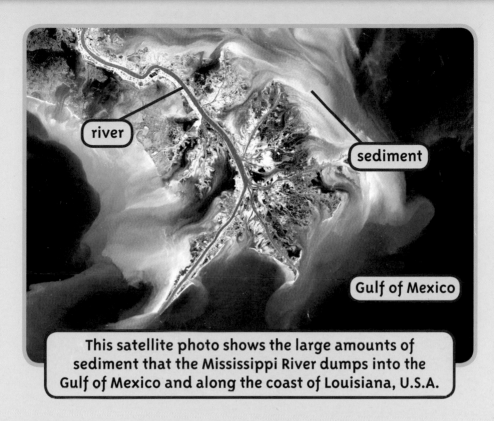

river

sediment

Gulf of Mexico

This satellite photo shows the large amounts of sediment that the Mississippi River dumps into the Gulf of Mexico and along the coast of Louisiana, U.S.A.

When a river reaches the ocean, its water suddenly slows down. And all of the sediment it has picked up falls to the seafloor.

Water Words

ERODE: To wear away

SEDIMENT: Bits of soil, sand, and rock that are picked up by rivers and dumped in the ocean

Did You Know . . .

Some of the salt in seawater comes from sediment that rivers pick up as they flow toward the ocean.

Round and Round

All the water in Earth's oceans, lakes, and rivers has been here for billions of years. But that doesn't mean it has always stayed the same.

Water is special. It's the only substance found naturally in three forms—solid, liquid, and gas. And it can easily change from one form to another.

Icicles are a solid form of water.

liquid water

From Gas to Liquid

Place an empty drinking glass in the freezer. After ten minutes, take the glass out and watch what happens. As warm water vapor in the air hits the cold glass, the vapor cools down and condenses. The drops of liquid water that you see on the glass came from the air around it.

When liquid water gets hot, it evaporates and forms water vapor.

Water Words

WATER VAPOR: The gas form of water

CONDENSE: To change from a gas to a liquid

EVAPORATE: To change from a liquid to a gas

The Water Cycle

Water doesn't stay in one place for long. It's always on the go, moving from oceans, lakes, and rivers to the air, to the land, and then back again. This process is called the water cycle.

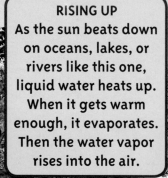

RISING UP
As the sun beats down on oceans, lakes, or rivers like this one, liquid water heats up. When it gets warm enough, it evaporates. Then the water vapor rises into the air.

It takes as many as 15 million tiny water droplets to form a raindrop large enough to fall to the ground.

CHILLING OUT
As the warm, moist air moves up, it starts to cool. Cool air can't hold as much moisture as warm air, so water vapor in the air condenses. It forms tiny water droplets.

FALLING DOWN
The water droplets bump into one another. They clump together to form clouds. The drops grow larger and larger, heavier and heavier, until they fall to the ground as rain or snow.

ROUND AND ROUND
Some of the rain and snow soaks into the ground. The rest lands in oceans, lakes, or rivers like this one. And the water cycle continues.

9 Cool Facts About Water

2 When ocean water evaporates, its salt gets left behind. That's one reason seawater is so salty.

1 More than two-thirds of the world's fresh water is locked up in glaciers.

3 Only half of the world's people have piped water in their homes.

4 A leaky faucet that loses a drop per second could fill 16 bathtubs in one month.

5

Water vapor usually stays in the air for less than two weeks.

6

Salt water freezes at a lower temperature than fresh water does.

7

The biggest snowflake on record fell in Montana in 1887. It was bigger than a dinner plate.

8

The energy in moving water can be used to make electricity.

9

During a downpour, rain may speed through the air at 20 miles an hour.

Water and Weather

The air around us contains a variety of different gases. But when it comes to weather, the most important gas is water vapor.

Water vapor can become the rain that ruins a picnic. It can become the snow that closes schools. That's why people check the weather report before deciding what clothes to wear and how to spend the day.

Near the Ground

On cool nights, water vapor near the ground condenses. It forms tiny water droplets.

When the tiny water droplets hang in the air, we see them as fog.

When the water vapor condenses on objects like grass, leaves, or a spider's web, we see dew.

If the nighttime temperature drops below the freezing point, the dew changes into a solid. The next morning, we see frost covering the grass.

Water Word

FREEZING POINT: The temperature at which liquid water changes to solid ice (32° Fahrenheit, 0° Celsius)

In the Sky

The air around Earth is full of water vapor. It's close to the ground, and it's high in the sky. When the water vapor above our heads condenses, we see clouds.

Clouds come in many different shapes and sizes. Some are miles and miles above the ground. Others are much closer.

Scientists divide clouds into three major groups: cirrus (SIR-us) clouds, cumulus (KYOOM-yuh-lus) clouds, and stratus (STRA-tuhs) clouds.

Cirrus Clouds

High, wispy cirrus clouds are usually a sign of good weather.

Cumulus Clouds

Puffy cumulus clouds can bring showers.

Stratus Clouds

Thick, low stratus clouds often cause a full day of rain and drizzle.

The Namib Desert in southern Africa gets less than a half inch of rain each year.

Too Much, Too Little

In some parts of the world, it rains almost every day. In other places, it hardly rains at all. The plants and animals in these areas know how to survive in their surroundings.

But sometimes a storm dumps too much rain. Rivers overflow and the land floods. The water can destroy homes and fields full of crops.

Other times, little or no rain falls on an area for weeks and weeks. This is called a drought (DROWT). Soil dries out and plants die. People may run out of water to drink. Too little rain can be just as damaging as too much rain.

Let It Snow

In winter, chilly air can freeze some of the tiny water droplets that make up a cloud. Nearby liquid droplets stick to the ice, and they freeze too.

As more and more droplets clump and freeze, the ice crystal grows heavier and heavier. Finally, it plunges downward.

Falling ice crystals collide and form snowflakes. By the time a flake hits the ground, it may contain thousands of crystals.

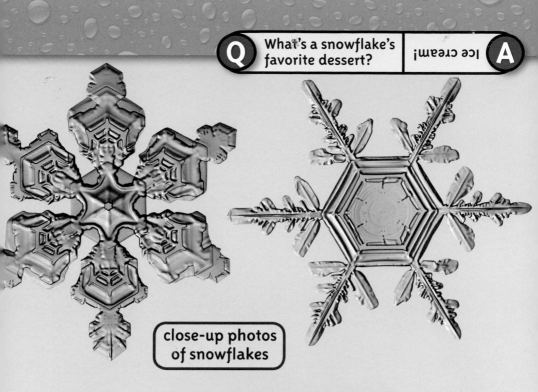

close-up photos
of snowflakes

Did You Know . . .

If falling snow starts to melt or mixes with rain, it becomes sleet.

If raindrops freeze as they hit the cold ground, they become freezing rain.

If whipping winds toss raindrops high into the sky, they can freeze solid and become hail.

Weird but true

A hailstone can be as big as a grapefruit.

Water in Your Body

Water isn't just an important part of our planet. It's an important part of your body, too. More than half of your total body weight is water. Your body uses water in all kinds of ways—from digesting food to getting rid of germs.

Your body loses water whenever you sweat or go to the bathroom. That's why you need to drink plenty of water every day.

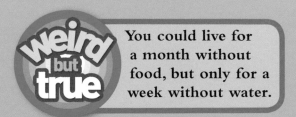

weird but true
You could live for a month without food, but only for a week without water.

Water in Your Life

You probably drink about a half gallon of water each day. But you also need water to clean your food, clothes, and body. Believe it or not, you probably use between 80 and 100 gallons of water every single day.

Think about all the ways your family uses water. Using the table below, work with an adult to add up how much water your family uses each week. Is it more than you expected?

Ways We Use Water at Home

Toilet flushing	About 6 gallons per flush
Shower	About 8 gallons per minute
Bath	About 40 gallons per bath
Washing machine	60 gallons per load
Dishwasher	15 gallons per load
Brushing teeth with tap running	10 gallons per brushing
Washing hands with tap running	2 gallons per washing

Water Warning

We drink water. We use it to cook, clean, and carry waste out of our homes. Farmers use it to grow crops, and companies use it to make products.

Since the 1950s, the amount of water people use has tripled. But the supply hasn't.

In some places, water is being used faster than it can be replaced. Scientists worry that soon there won't be enough water for us and the creatures that share our world.

What can you do to help?
Use water wisely.

Rain barrels collect and store water that runs off your roof. You can then use it to water plants or wash your car, saving up to 1,300 gallons of water during summer months.

Having enough water isn't our only problem. We also need to keep it clean.

Right now, ships are dumping trash into the ocean. Factories are pumping wastes into rivers and streams. Chemicals that farmers use to kill insects are draining into lakes and ponds. All this pollution can make the water dangerous to drink. It can also harm fish and other water creatures.

We need to work together to stop the pollution. It's the only way to protect our world's most precious natural resource.

Taking part in a local water cleanup day is one way to help reduce water pollution.

Water Words

POLLUTION: Harmful matter that makes water, soil, or air dirty

NATURAL RESOURCE: A material found in nature that is useful to humans

Be a Quiz Whiz!

How much do you know about water?
After reading this book, probably a lot!
Take this quiz and find out.

Answers are at the bottom of page 45.

The first life on Earth appeared in the ocean about _____ years ago.
A. 11,500
B. 326 million
C. 600 million
D. 3.5 billion

Which is the largest lake in North America?
A. Lake Michigan
B. Lake Superior
C. Lake Huron
D. Lake Erie

Rain and melting snow flow downhill until they finally reach _____ .
A. A stream
B. A puddle
C. The ocean
D. A river

4

What happens when water vapor cools down?
A. It evaporates.
B. It freezes.
C. It condenses.
D. It stays the same.

5

What can cause a full day of rain and drizzle?
A. Stratus clouds
B. Cumulus clouds
C. Cirrus clouds
D. Fog

6

How much of your total body weight is water?
A. Less than a quarter
B. More than half
C. Three-quarters
D. Almost all

7

What causes water pollution?
A. Ships dump trash into the ocean.
B. Factories pump wastes into rivers.
C. Chemicals drain into lakes and ponds.
D. All of the above

Glossary

CONDENSE: To change from a gas to a liquid

ERODE: To wear away

EVAPORATE: To change from a liquid to a gas

NATURAL RESOURCE: A material found in nature that is useful to humans

POLLUTION: Harmful matter that makes water, soil, or air dirty

CURRENT: A flowing stream of water within a larger body of water

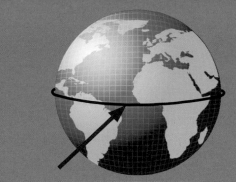

EQUATOR: An imaginary line around Earth halfway between the North and South Poles

FREEZING POINT: The temperature at which liquid water changes to solid ice (32° Fahrenheit, 0° Celsius)

GLACIER: A giant ice sheet that slowly moves out in all directions

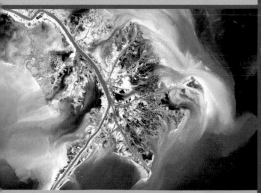

SEDIMENT: Bits of soil, sand, and rock that are picked up by rivers and dumped in the ocean

WATER VAPOR: The gas form of water

Index

Illustrations are indicated by **boldface.**